Praying
with the
Psalms

Praying *with the* Psalms

3-Minute Devotions for Lent and Holy Week 2026

EMILY MAE MENTOCK

AVE MARIA PRESS AVE Notre Dame, Indiana

Give thanks to the Lord, for he is good,
his mercy endures forever.
—Psalm 118

*The first psalm I fell in love with,
and the one that renews my hope
each time I hear it.*

Acknowledgments

I'm deeply grateful to Eric Clayton, whose invitation to write a simple Advent reflection in 2024 rekindled my creative spirit. My thanks also go to Eileen Ponder, editor of this series, for her confidence in my voice to accompany others on their Lenten journey and her guidance through the editing process. I'm indebted to Fr. Jean Corbon, the Lebanese Melkite priest who drafted the fourth pillar of the *Catechism of the Catholic Church* on Christian prayer; his profound catechesis on the book of Psalms awakened in me a deep love for them.

I certainly must thank my sister Maggie, her husband Jacob, and my own husband Andrew, for their support and encouragement throughout the writing of this devotional. And finally, I give thanks to God for the gift of this project. While I hope these reflections have touched your heart or supported your Lenten journey in some way, the opportunity to pray and reflect with the psalms has been a gift in and of itself—one I am grateful to have undertaken, even if no one else would benefit.

Introduction

The *Catechism of the Catholic Church* calls the psalms "the prayer of the assembly." In paragraph 2586, it says: "Their prayer recalls the saving events of the past, yet extends into the future, even to the end of history; it commemorates the promises God has already kept, and awaits the Messiah who will fulfill them definitively. Prayed by Christ and fulfilled in him, the Psalms remain essential to the prayer of the Church" (cf. *General Introduction to the Liturgy of the Hours*).

And yet, how often do we truly pay attention to the psalms at Mass? Sometimes it's hard, especially when we're at the mercy of a cantor's melody or delivery. And despite being the prayer of the assembly, we're rarely invited to participate in the singing or praying aloud of the verses ourselves. What an opportunity we have to rediscover them in a new way this Lent!

One of the reasons that I love the psalms is that they are honest! They are relatable and deeply human. They are the collective prayer of the Church and the personal cry of a soul seeking God. These are the prayers Jesus himself would have prayed.

Lent is challenging. In part because it requires endurance! Forty days (not including Sundays) is quite the marathon in a world where our attention is pulled in a thousand directions.

In this book, I reflect on just one or two lines from the psalm each day, letting them speak into our hearts and daily lives in just three minutes. But I encourage you to also read the full psalm chosen for Mass each day of Lent, ideally in your own Bible, not just from an online lectionary. Let it become personal—something to hold, to sit with and embrace.

When you finish the main part of the reflection and arrive at the call to "Rest in silence with the Lord," please do try to close your eyes and take a few breaths while inviting the Holy Spirit to stir within you. Try to get in touch with your heart—your inner dwelling place where God meets you—before you move on to the final reflection question.

My hope is that each day of this Lenten journey leaves you feeling seen, affirmed, challenged, and filled with hope as you grow closer to God through the words of the psalms until Easter.

Ash Wednesday

+ Have mercy on me, O God, in your goodness.

A clean heart create for me, O God;
renew within me a steadfast spirit.
—Psalm 51:12

Every year, Lent comes as a gentle but necessary wake-up call. No matter how well I've started the year (usually more of a struggle than I'd like to admit), it reminds me that I can't rely on my own strength to grow closer to God. I will fail. I will sin. And I need God's forgiveness and grace to keep going.

The psalmist's prayer echoes the longing of all who come to receive ashes today. It's not just a plea for a fresh start and a clean heart, but a plea for the steadfast spirit we need to remain true to the God who saves us.

On Ash Wednesday, we come before God not merely out of an obligation to repent and seek renewal, but with our hearts open, longing to restore our relationships with him. The psalmist acknowledges sin honestly, recognizing that only God can cleanse and renew. We are called to do the same during this holy season.

Rest in silence with the Lord.

Today, as you wear your ashes, ask God for a spirit of true repentance and the grace to detach from sin this Lent so that you might grow closer to Christ.

A clean heart create for me, O God;
renew within me a steadfast spirit.

+ Have mercy on me, O God, in your goodness.

Week of Ash Wednesday

+ Have mercy on me, O God, in your goodness.

> Blessed is the one who does not walk
> in the counsel of the wicked,
> Nor stand in the way of sinners . . . .
> Rather, the law of the LORD is his joy;
> and on his law he meditates day and night.
> —Psalm 1:1–2

When you think about the "law of the LORD," do you think of it as a source of joy? God's law is not a burden but a gift, providing a clear path for our weak and wandering hearts. The *Catechism* tells us that help comes to man "in Christ through the law that guides him and the grace that sustains him" (*CCC* 1949).

On the path of the law, we won't just survive; we will thrive. We will bear fruit in due season. So don't lose heart if the results aren't immediate. And the best news? God didn't just hand us the law and leave us on our own. The Lord watches over us, ready to send the Holy Spirit to guide us. This is why we truly can find joy in the law.

Rest in silence with the Lord.

Where in the practice of your faith do you find joy? How can you magnify that joy today?

> Blessed is the one who does not walk
> in the counsel of the wicked,
> Nor stand in the way of sinners . . . .
> Rather, the law of the LORD is his joy;
> and on his law he meditates day and night.

+ Have mercy on me, O God, in your goodness.

Week of Ash Wednesday

+ Have mercy on me, O God, in your goodness.

My sacrifice, O God, is a contrite spirit;
a contrite, humbled heart, O God,
you will not scorn.
—Psalm 51:19

I have a faint memory of my First Reconciliation in second grade. I wish I could remember what I confessed. How did it feel? Did I leave with a sense that all my sins had been forgiven through the grace of this new-to-me sacrament? Or did I simply recite a list of sins suggested by my religion textbook?

Now, as an adult, I am much more aware that a truly contrite heart is a required disposition to receive the graces of the sacrament. Forgiveness isn't a mere transaction for saying "sorry." It is a grace-filled response to a contrite heart that seeks genuine reconciliation with God and with others. We must also remember that God is Truth. To draw closer to God, we must live in his truth, most especially in our relationship with him.

Rest in silence with the Lord.

Today, make a commitment to receive the Sacrament of Reconciliation this Lent. Ask for the grace to do so with a truly contrite heart.

My sacrifice, O God, is a contrite spirit;
a contrite, humbled heart, O God,
you will not scorn.

+ Have mercy on me, O God, in your goodness.

Saturday, February 21

Week of Ash Wednesday

+ Have mercy on me, O God, in your goodness.

Be gracious to me, Lord;
to you I call all the day.
—Psalm 86:3

How often do we lift our hearts to God throughout an ordinary day? For every time I text a friend or scroll through Instagram, how many times do I turn to God instead? The psalms teach us to bring everything to God—our joys, sorrows, and longings. Fasting isn't just self-denial; it's a reordering of our hearts, making space for God to fill us. Every craving we encounter while fasting becomes an opportunity to turn to him in prayer.

Last year, I gave up desserts for Lent. It wasn't a huge sacrifice, but I noticed how often I longed for something sweet. Each craving became a choice: Would I dwell on what I was missing, or let my hunger lead me to God? Instead of grumbling, I prayed, "Lord, be my joy. Satisfy me more than any worldly sweetness ever could."

Lent isn't about sacrifice alone—it's about letting every longing draw us closer to the One who truly satisfies. The next time we feel tempted, let our hearts echo the psalms and turn to God instead. He will not disappoint.

Rest in silence with the Lord.

Try to keep track of how many times you call upon God in a day and do your best to stay close to him. Reflect on the outcome of this activity. How did it make you feel?

Be gracious to me, Lord;
to you I call all the day.

+ Have mercy on me, O God, in your goodness.

First Week of Lent

+ Out of the depths I cry to you, O Lord; hear my voice!

Restore to me the gladness of your salvation;
uphold me with a willing spirit.
—Psalm 51:14

Do you know that feeling when the sun finally breaks through the clouds, and you instinctively turn your face toward it, soaking in its warmth and light? That's what Sundays feel like during Lent. They are mini feast days, breaths of fresh air, and reminders of the joy in God's loving plan for our salvation.

Today at Mass, we hear about Jesus's temptation in the desert. We also hear the psalmist crying out for something we all need: the joy of salvation and a willing spirit to pursue it. It's like the start of a race. Those first few miles feel great, but the moment it gets hard, reality sets in. It's going to take endurance. Before thinking you have to run this race alone, remember that the Holy Spirit gives life and sustains our relationship with God. We are meant to call upon the Spirit for strength.

Let Sundays refresh you. Let joy sustain you. And never forget that we are running toward the ultimate hope of our salvation, Jesus's Resurrection.

Rest in silence with the Lord.

How can you embrace the joy of the Lord's Day to sustain you through the coming week of Lent?

Restore to me the gladness of your salvation;
uphold me with a willing spirit.

+ Out of the depths I cry to you, O Lord; hear my voice!

First Week of Lent

+ Out of the depths I cry to you, O LORD; hear my voice!

The decree of the LORD is trustworthy,
giving wisdom to the simple.
—Psalm 19:8

Do you ever reach a point in your day or week when things get tough, and you find yourself asking God, *Is this really what I'm supposed to be doing?* Whether in family matters, friendships, parish, neighborhood relations, workplace, or school, you're not alone if you question God's plan for you in difficult moments. Even during Lent, when faced with your own imperfections, you might wonder, *Is holiness really for me?* But the psalmist assures us today that more than anyone or anything else, God is worthy of our trust. He loves us beyond measure and desires that we have a fruitful Lent more than we can possibly imagine.

There are many sources of wisdom within our Catholic Church. If you haven't yet read the Holy Father's message for Lent this year or his homily from yesterday, today is a great day to do so. Let it renew our faithfulness to whatever God is asking of us right now.

Rest in silence with the Lord.

Recall a time when you struggled to trust that you were where God wanted you to be. How can you renew your faithfulness to God's plan, even when the path feels uncertain?

The decree of the LORD is trustworthy,
giving wisdom to the simple.

+ Out of the depths I cry to you, O LORD; hear my voice!

First Week of Lent

+ Out of the depths I cry to you, O LORD; hear my voice!

The LORD is close to the brokenhearted;
saves those whose spirit is crushed.
—Psalm 34:19

This is one of my favorite lines in all of scripture; it has been a source of consolation to me countless times. In a fallen world, we get our hearts broken. And not just in the romantic sense—sometimes life itself and the people in it break our hearts. Sometimes it's getting passed over for a promotion or the words of a frustrated barista. Sometimes we break our own hearts by putting our hope and trust in people and things other than God.

Each year around this point in Lent, if I've been faithful to my spiritual practices, I begin to recognize some deeper brokenness starting to surface within myself. That's how God works when we give him even a small part of our hearts to heal, maybe even the part that longs for chocolate. In his infinite goodness and generous love, God goes deeper in transforming us. But never further than we can handle. If you're like me and this first week of Lent is hitting a little harder than you expected, don't despair. Listen to the psalmist today.

Rest in silence with the Lord.

Where in your life have you placed your hope and trust in something other than God? How might you invite Christ into your brokenness this Lent, allowing his love to heal and restore you?

The LORD is close to the brokenhearted;
saves those whose spirit is crushed.

+ Out of the depths I cry to you, O LORD; hear my voice!

First Week of Lent

+ Out of the depths I cry to you, O LORD; hear my voice!

For you do not desire sacrifice, or I would give it;
a burnt offering you would not accept.
—Psalm 51:18

One week in, do you feel as if your Lenten practice is changing you? Maybe your fasting isn't challenging enough, or maybe you haven't followed through on your intention for almsgiving. But as the psalmist reminds us today, we aren't doing these practices just for the sake of rituals.

I remember one Lent when I tried to give up social media for personal use while still being on Twitter and Instagram every day for work. Hardly a sacrifice! The experience reminded me that the only sacrifice God truly wants is one that changes us for the better. While sacrifice does mean offering to God what belongs to him, let's not mistake that for thinking he is "owed" the discomfort that giving up dessert or social media might cause us. God doesn't want that; he wants our hearts. He created us to love him, and that's what we owe him.

Rest in silence with the Lord.

Are you using your Lenten sacrifices to check a box and keep a tradition, or are you truly giving your heart over to God in an effort to cleanse it and restore your relationship with him?

For you do not desire sacrifice, or I would give it;
a burnt offering you would not accept.

+ Out of the depths I cry to you, O LORD; hear my voice!

First Week of Lent

+ Out of the depths I cry to you, O Lord; hear my voice!

I thank you, Lord, with all my heart;
in the presence of the angels to you I sing.
—Psalm 138:1

We Catholics recognize five types of prayer: blessing or adoration, petition, intercession, thanksgiving, and praise. During Lent, my prayer tends to focus on petition: asking God for mercy and for help in navigating the challenges of this season. As my prayer discipline strengthens over these Lenten days, I also notice an increase in intercession, lifting up prayers for others.

But just because it's Lent doesn't mean we should hesitate to give God thanks and praise! As we hear at Mass, "It is truly right and just, . . . always and everywhere to give you thanks." This, of course, includes during Lent! So today, instead of focusing only on our need for God's generosity and mercy, take some time to praise him for who he is and give thanks for all the good he has done for you.

Rest in silence with the Lord.

Which type of prayer comes most naturally to you, and which do you tend to overlook? How can you intentionally incorporate more thanksgiving and praise into your prayer this Lent?

I thank you, Lord, with all my heart;
in the presence of the angels to you I sing.

+ Out of the depths I cry to you, O Lord; hear my voice!

Friday, February 27

First Week of Lent

+ Out of the depths I cry to you, O Lord; hear my voice!

I wait for the Lord,
my soul waits, and I hope for his word.
My soul looks for the Lord
more than sentinels for daybreak.
—Psalm 130:5–6

Spiritual discipline is important in times of discernment, and Lent naturally lends itself to that. I also think that with the changing seasons comes a certain restlessness, or perhaps simply a greater openness to change in our lives.

Should I change jobs? Should I use my summer vacation to visit my grandmother, or take a trip with a friend? Or the even bigger question: *God, what do you want me to do with my life this year?* I often begin Lent eagerly waiting for the answer. I hope to hear from God. And usually, around this time, I start wondering if I'm going to hear anything. But today, the psalmist reminds us to wait patiently for God. His word is stronger than our feelings, and we shouldn't rush to plan our lives without him. Our minds may be ready to make a decision and move on, but our souls long for God more than anything. We need to wait.

Rest in silence with the Lord.

Where in your life are you seeking answers from God? How can you practice both patience with and trust in his timing?

I wait for the Lord,
my soul waits, and I hope for his word.
My soul looks for the Lord
more than sentinels for daybreak.

+ Out of the depths I cry to you, O Lord; hear my voice!

First Week of Lent

+ Out of the depths I cry to you, O Lord; hear my voice!

Blessed those whose way is blameless,
who walk by the law of the Lord.
Blessed those who keep his testimonies,
who seek him with all their heart.
—Psalm 119:1–2

Blameless? That's a tough standard to meet! Thank goodness the psalmist goes further to clarify what he means: those who walk in the way of the Lord. Our ways could never be blameless, but God's ways always are. He doesn't expect us to be perfect, but he created us to follow him. And when we walk in his ways, we find the greatest blessings of our lives. Sometimes, it's a struggle to stay true to the law of the Lord, but God never turns his back on those who seek him, even when we struggle or fail.

More than anything, God wants us to seek him with all our hearts, and Lent is the perfect time to practice giving more and more of our hearts to this pursuit. As our fasting and almsgiving help us detach from the things of this world, let's allow our hearts to return to God and walk by his law.

Rest in silence with the Lord.

Where in your life are you tempted to follow your own way instead of God's law of love? How might you use this Lenten season to realign your heart with God's path?

Blessed those whose way is blameless,
who walk by the law of the Lord.
Blessed those who keep his testimonies,
who seek him with all their heart.

+ Out of the depths I cry to you, O Lord; hear my voice!

Sunday, March 1

Second Week of Lent

+ Lord, let your mercy be upon us, as we place our trust in you.

He loves justice and right.
The earth is full of the mercy of the Lord.
—Psalm 33:5

I just love the idea of God loving something, don't you? This line from Psalm 33 always makes me pause and wonder: When God looks at our world, what moments and places make him smile? It stirs in me a childlike sense of awe—imagining God watching over the whole world, yet still seeing each and every one of us, just as we are.

Where there is goodness, there is God. His love is not distant or abstract; it's all around us where people are doing good. So, if you're searching for God in the world, start there. And if you're searching for God's presence in your own life, consider how you might be kinder, more just, and more "right." You won't be disappointed because God will be right there with you. His kingdom comes to life in this world through us.

Rest in silence with the Lord.

Where does God see "justice and right" in you? Where might he be inviting you to bring his kindness into the world?

He loves justice and right.
The earth is full of the mercy of the Lord.

+ Lord, let your mercy be upon us, as we place our trust in you.

Second Week of Lent

+ Lord, let your mercy be upon us, as we place our trust in you.

> Then we, your people, the sheep of your pasture,
> will give thanks to you forever;
> from generation to generation
> we will recount your praise.
> —Psalm 79:13

The pasture mentioned by the psalmist today is an interesting image because we've always been free to wander away. But now, thanks to the sacrifice of God's only Son, we are also free to return to him. This is why we will give thanks forever: because it is the greatest gift in the world. This Lent, I want to focus on the pasture I've been given and the shepherd who watches over me. I pray that I will stay within his care, not only to be saved from death but to be freed from my sins. This is not a one-time decision but a daily choice to turn back, to remain in his pasture, and to give thanks to the one who leads us home.

Rest in silence with the Lord.

In what areas of your life have you wandered from God's care? How can you make the daily choice to return to him and remain in his pasture?

> Then we, your people, the sheep of your pasture,
> will give thanks to you forever;
> from generation to generation
> we will recount your praise.

+ Lord, let your mercy be upon us, as we place our trust in you.

Second Week of Lent

+ LORD, let your mercy be upon us, as we place our trust in you.

> When you do these things should I be silent?
> Do you think that I am like you?
> I accuse you, I lay out the matter before your eyes.
> —Psalm 50:21

It's important to note that the psalmist is speaking in God's voice in this verse, since this might be easy to miss. God's words here are powerful. How often do we sin by assuming he is like us, rather than remembering that we are made to be like God? One of my favorite reminders from the *Catechism of the Catholic Church*, 2779, is "We must humbly cleanse our hearts of certain false images drawn 'from this world.'"

How many times have I struggled to believe in God's mercy because I struggle to be merciful? Or doubted his love because I fail to love others as I should? Too many times for certain! Next time you question or simply forget God's infiniteness, ask him to show you who he *really* is.

Rest in silence with the Lord.

Where in your life have you projected your own limitations onto God? How can you open your heart to see him as he truly is, rather than as you imagine him to be?

> When you do these things should I be silent?
> Do you think that I am like you?
> I accuse you, I lay out the matter before your eyes.

+ LORD, let your mercy be upon us, as we place our trust in you.

Second Week of Lent

+ LORD, let your mercy be upon us, as we place our trust in you.

Free me from the net they have set for me,
for you are my refuge.
—Psalm 31:5

During some of my more tumultuous years as a teenager and college student, there were many days I spent curled up in a particular armchair. After a hard day, I would come home, sit there, and think. I cried through breakups in that chair. I wrestled with uncertainty about my future in that chair. Even though some of my hardest moments are tied to that place, in many ways, it was my safe place. But while that chair provided an escape from the world, it couldn't offer me real refuge. At the time, I didn't have much of a relationship with God, although I wish I had. I wish I had known I could turn to him instead of turning inward, carrying those burdens alone.

The psalmist understood something I didn't back then: God is our true and lasting refuge. No matter how trapped we feel—by the weight of the world or even by our own sins—God can free us. And he will welcome you into the only truly lasting safe place: his love.

Rest in silence with the Lord.

Where in your life do you feel trapped, and how can you invite God to be your refuge and sure source of freedom?

Free me from the net they have set for me,
for you are my refuge.

+ LORD, let your mercy be upon us, as we place our trust in you.

Second Week of Lent

+ Lord, let your mercy be on us, as we place our trust in you.

> He is like a tree planted near streams of water,
> that yields its fruit in season;
> Its leaves never wither; whatever he does prospers.
> —Psalm 1:3

I'll be honest with you—when I woke up this morning, I did not feel like a tree whose leaves never fade. I was grumbling about my to-do list, focused on myself, and then I remembered my usual morning prayer: thanking God for the day, inviting him into it, and asking what he wants of me.

Now, maybe this isn't exactly what the psalmist meant by a person who delights in the law of the Lord and meditates on it day and night! Clearly, I missed the morning part. But I do think it reflects a desire to delight in God's ways. The tree in the psalm isn't planted *in* the water; it's near the water, able to draw sustenance from it. The *Catechism* teaches that the "wellsprings" of prayer come from the Holy Spirit and the Church. How many of us have planted ourselves near these life-giving sources?

We can be that tree if we choose to build up our spiritual life. And in due time—maybe by Easter, maybe when we least expect it—we will bear good fruit.

Rest in silence with the Lord.

Where is God inviting you to root yourself more deeply in his love?

> He is like a tree planted near streams of water,
> that yields its fruit in season;
> Its leaves never wither; whatever he does prospers.

+ Lord, let your mercy be upon us, as we place our trust in you.

Second Week of Lent

+ LORD, let your mercy be upon us, as we place our trust in you.

> He rescued me from my mighty enemy,
> from foes too powerful for me.
> They attacked me on my day of distress,
> but the LORD was my support.
> —Psalm 18:18–19

Today's psalm verses recall the story of Joseph, whose brothers sold him into slavery—until God delivered him because of his faithfulness. It's one of the most well-known and retold stories of the Old Testament, and for good reason.

Joseph was faithful and prospered, just like our tree from yesterday. But then, he was betrayed by those who were supposed to love him and found himself alone in a desperate situation. Most of us will never suffer in that way, but I'm sure you can think of a time when it felt like the world had turned against you. How did you respond? Joseph chose to keep trusting in God. And God did not disappoint him.

This is an Old Testament story, but perhaps the words that are more familiar come from St. Paul: *Hope does not disappoint.* So today, no matter what the world throws at you, stay close to God.

Rest in silence with the Lord.

Where will you allow yourself to hope today?

> He rescued me from my mighty enemy,
> from foes too powerful for me.
> They attacked me on my day of distress,
> but the LORD was my support.

+ LORD, let your mercy be upon us, as we place our trust in you.

Second Week of Lent

+ Lord, let your mercy be upon us, as we place our trust in you.

Bless the Lord, my soul; . . .
Who redeems your life from the pit,
and crowns you with mercy and compassion.
—Psalm 103:2, 4

When I'm stressed, I am not at my best. I can be short with others, and I start to only focus on my own life and problems. Before long, it feels like everything is falling apart—even when it's not!

God doesn't want us to live that way, and he gives us the virtues of faith, hope, and love to redeem us from destruction—whether from real challenges or drama of our own making. Whatever struggles we're facing, God wants to save us from them. We should turn to him as our Savior. What we'll find is that by clinging to trust in God's saving power, we'll gain the strength to face any challenge. We'll begin to look beyond ourselves and return to the kindness and compassion that flow naturally from the peace of trusting in the Lord.

Rest in silence with the Lord.

Where in your life do you need to let go and trust God more fully?

Bless the Lord, my soul; . . .
Who redeems your life from the pit,
and crowns you with mercy and compassion.

+ Lord, let your mercy be upon us, as we place our trust in you.

Third Week of Lent

+ My soul longs for you, O God.

Let us come before him with a song of praise,
joyfully sing out our psalms.
—Psalm 95:2

We made it to another Sunday! I couldn't help but choose this line from today's psalm as the focus of reflection. I remember when I first truly discovered the psalms—it completely transformed how I experienced them at Mass. I started following along with the verses, either in the hymnal or on my phone, so I could actually pay attention to the words the cantor was singing. And as I became more familiar with the psalms and deepened my relationship with God through them, I found myself singing with more wholehearted participation.

Have you had that experience yet in the first two weeks of Lent? It's okay if you feel self-conscious about your singing, but you don't need to be: The psalmist says nothing about talent, but rather, invites us to sing joyfully! If we are to come into God's presence with songs of praise, what better place than the celebration of the Eucharist, our great liturgy of praise and thanksgiving?

Rest in silence with the Lord.

How can you more fully engage with the psalms and the Mass, allowing both to deepen your gratitude and draw you closer to God?

Let us come before him with a song of praise,
joyfully sing out our psalms.

+ My soul longs for you, O God.

Third Week of Lent

+ My soul longs for you, O God.

Send your light and your fidelity,
that they may be my guide;
Let them bring me to your holy mountain,
to the place of your dwelling.
—Psalm 43:3

I'm not an avid runner, but I enjoy the occasional 5 or 10K race. One trick I've learned—especially when running without much training—is that it's so much easier to follow someone else's pace than to set my own. The difference in mental effort is incredible. I can run faster, last longer, and feel stronger when I follow a runner who's clearly more experienced than I am.

The same is true in our journey through life and, hopefully, to heaven. We can try to lead ourselves through the ups and downs of our relationships with God, relying on our own broken, human hearts. But that path is more exhausting, frustrating, and disappointing than simply letting God lead. So stop trying to force your own way! Let the Lord set the pace and the route. If you trust in God's loving light and perfect faithfulness, he will carry you farther than you ever imagined.

Rest in silence with the Lord.

Think about a step you can take this Lent to surrender to God and trust him to guide you.

Send your light and your fidelity,
that they may be my guide;
Let them bring me to your holy mountain,
to the place of your dwelling.

+ My soul longs for you, O God.

Third Week of Lent

+ My soul longs for you, O God.

He guides the humble in righteousness,
and teaches the humble his way.
—Psalm 25:9

My sister and I used to ride a tandem bike around our neighborhood. Both seats had handlebars, but only the front ones were meant to steer. Of course, whoever was in the back couldn't help but try to take control, which inevitably led to a crash. The one in the back had to learn to stop gripping the handlebars, stop trying to steer, and trust the one who was meant to lead.

Why does the Lord guide and teach the humble? Because only the humble can be taught! Sometimes we think, *Okay, God, I'm ready for you to lead*—only to find ourselves acting like a backseat driver, throwing everything off course. But God, in his goodness, patiently waits until we are truly ready to be led. And that requires humility.

This Lent, instead of clinging to control and wandering aimlessly in the desert, seek humility—maybe by praying the Litany of Humility—and let the Holy Spirit be your guide.

Rest in silence with the Lord.

How can you practice humility and trust in his guidance this Lent?

He guides the humble in righteousness,
and teaches the humble his way.

+ My soul longs for you, O God.

Third Week of Lent

+ My soul longs for you, O God.

He sends forth his command to earth;
his word runs swiftly!
—Psalm 147:15

Have you ever sent up a petition to God, only to shrug it off, thinking, *he's probably not going to answer this anyway?* Me too, friend. But that couldn't be further from the truth! Not only does God listen to our prayers, but also we should expect an answer. God is present, and the Holy Spirit is actively at work in both our world and our lives.

Today's psalm verse points us toward the many good things God has done for Israel, but this isn't just a story from the past. Even now, God sends forth his commands into the world. And unlike earthly powers, when God speaks, his word works. So, ask God to move in your life. Recall his goodness, trust in his faithfulness, and lift up your petition with expectant hope. He has worked wonders before, and he is still working them now.

Rest in silence with the Lord.

Do you truly believe that God hears and answers your prayers? Practice approaching God with greater trust and expectant hope.

He sends forth his command to earth;
his word runs swiftly!

+ My soul longs for you, O God.

Third Week of Lent

+ My soul longs for you, O God.

Do not harden your hearts as at Meribah,
as on the day of Massah in the desert.
There your ancestors tested me;
they tried me though they had seen my works.
—Psalm 95:8–9

My sister blessed me with a sweet little niece about a year ago, and I have loved having this amazing little person in my life! But one thing I've learned is that I can't make her love me. Even after the best day together, I might go in for a hug or high-five the next day, only for her to turn away. That's part of being a one-year-old, and part of being an aunt, I guess!

In today's psalm, we hear God's voice responding to the Israelites doing the very same thing. They knew his love, yet they turned away and tested him anyway. And now, God is saying to us: Don't be like them.

Rest in silence with the Lord.

When have you hardened your heart against love, peace, or mercy? Remember, God *is* love. He longs to dwell in your heart and find love there.

Do not harden your hearts as at Meribah,
as on the day of Massah in the desert.
There your ancestors tested me;
they tried me though they had seen my works.

+ My soul longs for you, O God.

Third Week of Lent

+ My soul longs for you, O God.

O that my people would listen to me,
that Israel would walk in my ways.
—Psalm 81:14

One time, after sharing all the times throughout my day when I called on God (asking him to bless my work, to send the Holy Spirit, to guide my decisions, etc.), my spiritual director asked me, "And does God respond?" It was the million-dollar question because I had sought out a spiritual director precisely to better hear God's voice. There were areas in my life where I felt blocked from hearing it. The truth that both my spiritual director and I knew is this: God does respond. In fact, he calls first! Our entire life is an invitation to respond to him. So why is it that, at times, we struggle to hear his voice?

A good place to start is by seeking out the places where we know we can hear him. Scripture, of course, is one. Being in the Real Presence of Jesus in the Eucharist is another. Recently, I have taken up journaling again as a spiritual practice to better hear him. Since we are made in his image, we can hear even God within ourselves. I encourage you to try journaling, too!

Rest in silence with the Lord.

Where can you go today to better hear God's voice?

O that my people would listen to me,
that Israel would walk in my ways.

+ My soul longs for you, O God.

Third Week of Lent

+ My soul longs for you, O God.

Treat Zion kindly according to your good will;
build up the walls of Jerusalem.
—Psalm 51:20

Most people don't think of Lent as a bountiful season. The spiritual desert we are called to enter in the first days of Lent can feel barren and dry. But as you strip away the usual pleasures and comforts of the world, God's grace abounds!

One place where this bounty becomes evident is in the rebuilding and repairing of relationships. Prayer, fasting, and almsgiving are meant to reorder our relationships with God, ourselves, and others. As you go deeper into Lent and experience this renewal, do you recognize it as God's abundant kindness?

Twice in my life, I've had the privilege of being in the California desert during a super bloom. It was incredible. But here's the thing—the desert only bloomed what was already there, waiting through the drought and dust until an abundance of rain brought it to life. That's how I imagine the bounty of God's grace on the Lenten journey.

Rest in silence with the Lord.

Which areas of your life are waiting for God's bounty to be poured into?

Treat Zion kindly according to your good will;
build up the walls of Jerusalem.

+ My soul longs for you, O God.

Sunday, March 15

Fourth Week of Lent

+ The Lord is gracious and merciful.

> Even though I walk through the valley
> of the shadow of death,
> I will fear no evil, for you are with me;
> your rod and your staff comfort me.
> —Psalm 23:4

In the aftermath of a harsh betrayal by a friend, I found myself one evening feeling particularly alone and upset. This wasn't only because of the betrayal itself but because the situation seemed to be working out for everyone but me. How could God allow such an injustice? I felt the darkness of the world creeping into my heart. I told God that I felt abandoned. Then, I felt a wave of shame. How could I dare use the same words Jesus spoke from the Cross?

But God the Father, who never abandons us, gently placed the words of this psalm on my heart. It was as if he was whispering, "I am with you. You only need to turn and look for me." Comfort washed over me. It was a powerful experience of the psalmist's promise: Even in the valley of the shadow of death—or any lesser trial!—we need not fear. Look up. Fix your gaze on our shepherd and let his staff comfort you, and you will be okay.

Rest in silence with the Lord.

When have you felt abandoned or overwhelmed by fear? How might God be inviting you to trust him in similar situations?

> Even though I walk through the valley
> of the shadow of death,
> I will fear no evil, for you are with me;
> your rod and your staff comfort me.

+ The Lord is gracious and merciful.

Fourth Week of Lent

+ The Lord is gracious and merciful.

You changed my mourning into dancing.
—Psalm 30:12

I love this line from the psalmist because of its vivid word choice. He's talking about actions, not just feelings. It doesn't say "sadness into happiness" because God doesn't control our emotions. Instead, he gives us grace, and we are invited to cooperate with it.

It reminds me of the times I've chosen to remain in mourning—not only in moments of grief, but also in less serious situations such as times when I held onto a complaining attitude or chose to wallow in self-pity. But God invites us to something greater and calls us to trust his message of good news: that he sent his Son out of love for us, and that the Father and the Son send the Holy Spirit to guide us. With the Spirit, we can choose gratitude instead of complaining. We can choose to give instead of wallow. We can choose to dance instead of mourn.

When you feel down, heartbroken, or simply discouraged, don't be afraid to ask God to remind you how deeply he loves you, how much you can trust him, and how much you still have to hope for.

Rest in silence with the Lord.

What would it look like for you to choose dancing over mourning in your life right now?

You changed my mourning into dancing.

+ The Lord is gracious and merciful.

Fourth Week of Lent

+ The Lord is gracious and merciful.

The Lord of hosts is with us;
our stronghold is the God of Jacob.
—Psalm 46:8

One time, I was traveling alone when a good friend suggested that I meet up with another friend of hers who happened to be in the same city I was. I had never met this friend-of-a-friend before, but I was confident we'd have a great time together. Why? Because I knew *my* friend well. I'd heard stories from her college days—stories that included this other friend—and that was all the endorsement I needed.

Sometimes, scripture introduces God in a similar way. Our psalm verse today begins with, "The Lord of hosts is with us." This title emphasizes God's almighty power and his command over heavenly armies; it shows how big God is. But that can feel distant. The psalmist brings it closer to home and gives us a more personal understanding of who this is: the God of Jacob. That's when we think, *Oh, that God! The one who promised Jacob land and descendants, who remained faithful, who changed his name to Israel. That* God is our stronghold. And *that* God is with us today.

Rest in silence with the Lord.

What helps you feel a personal connection with God or reminds you that you can trust him completely?

The Lord of hosts is with us;
our stronghold is the God of Jacob.

+ The Lord is gracious and merciful.

Fourth Week of Lent

+ The Lord is gracious and merciful.

The Lord is good to all,
compassionate toward all your works.
—Psalm 145:9

I recently listened to a podcast featuring a therapist (who wasn't Christian) who discouraged compassion. She reasoned that compassion makes you vulnerable and leads to your being taken advantage of or hurt again. I found myself frustrated by what I heard, realizing she had a fundamental misunderstanding of what compassion truly is.

Compassion means to "suffer with." It's not merely kindness or a naive sense of obligation.

Why does God need to be compassionate toward our works? Because, friends, we are all suffering. Whether from the brokenness of the world, past wounds, or our own human flaws, we all carry pain. And no matter how hard we try, we struggle. We fall short. Only God is perfect. Which makes it all the more incredible that he chooses to suffer with us. When we come up short, God doesn't dismiss us as not good enough. He sees our struggles and our suffering—and responds with grace, mercy, and love.

Rest in silence with the Lord.

Where in your life do you need to be reminded that God sees your struggle and responds with compassion? Let that inspire you to renew your commitment to pursuing goodness.

The Lord is good to all,
compassionate toward all your works.

+ The Lord is gracious and merciful.

Thursday, March 19
Fourth Week of Lent

Solemnity of Saint Joseph

+ The Lord is gracious and merciful.

I will sing of your mercy forever, Lord
proclaim your faithfulness through all ages.
—Psalm 89:2

I've always found ancient stories passed down through oral tradition to be especially fascinating. What strikes me as particularly beautiful is that these stories weren't just a way to teach the next generation; they helped the entire community remember together. I've found this to be true in my own life, too. The stories I share most often are the ones I remember most vividly. They're the ones that shape the narrative I live by.

It's not perfect, but in many ways, we can choose what we remember. So, if you're struggling to recall who God is or what his love has done in your life, pause to remember. Think of a time you experienced his mercy. Tell yourself the story again. Try writing it down, saying it aloud to yourself, or retelling it to Jesus during adoration. You're proclaiming truth to God and to your own heart, and you'll be amazed at what you rediscover.

Rest in silence with the Lord.

What story of God's mercy in your life do you need to retell today and how might sharing it help you rediscover God's faithfulness?

I will sing of your mercy forever, Lord
proclaim your faithfulness through all ages.

+ The Lord is gracious and merciful.

Fourth Week of Lent

+ The Lord is gracious and merciful.

Many are the troubles of the righteous,
but the Lord delivers him from them all.
—Psalm 34:20

I love when the Bible or the *Catechism* keeps it real. As much as I love Psalm 1 and its description of the joy and prosperity of those who follow the law of the Lord (which is true!), there are times when, in the face of adversity, I struggle to relate to that joyful image. Today's psalm verse acknowledges a reassuring truth: Many are the troubles of the righteous. And Jesus echoed the same message when he told his disciples they would be persecuted.

Now, most of us reading this don't face persecution like Christians of ancient times or today in other parts of the world. But I've certainly experienced unfair judgment, unkind mockery, or even subtle forms of prejudice in response to my public witness of faith. And, to be honest, I've also let fear hold me back from being as courageous in my faith as I'd like to be. But as the psalmist tells us today, the Lord delivers the righteous from all their troubles. God's ways are often mysterious, and we may not always understand how he's working. But we can trust that he will deliver us, as long as we keep pursuing him.

Rest in silence with the Lord.

What troubles or fears are holding you back in your faith right now? Can you step forward with courage, trusting that God will deliver you?

Many are the troubles of the righteous,
but the Lord delivers him from them all.

+ The Lord is gracious and merciful.

Fourth Week of Lent

+ The Lord is gracious and merciful.

Judge me, Lord, according to my righteousness,
and my integrity.
—Psalm 7:9

Lent is a time of repentance, but repentance doesn't end with acknowledging our sins. It calls for a full turning toward God, a movement forward with renewed clarity, commitment, and trust. It means believing in the Gospel—the Good News. And what is that Good News? That Jesus came to heal and to save.

Through the psalm verse for today, we boldly ask God to look at our righteousness and integrity. This isn't about pretending we are without sin; it's about trusting that God sees the good he has planted in our hearts and that he rejoices when we act with love and faithfulness. Interestingly, "Lent" means "spring." And what comes with spring? New life. New growth. As we draw near to Easter, may we be attentive to the signs of growth God is bringing about in our lives. Don't be afraid to bring your best to God, who delights in the goodness he sees in you.

Rest in silence with the Lord.

Where do you see signs of new growth in your spiritual life this Lent, and how can you continue turning toward God with greater trust and integrity?

Judge me, Lord, according to my righteousness,
and my integrity.

+ The Lord is gracious and merciful.

Sunday, March 22

Fifth Week of Lent

+ With the Lord there is mercy and fullness of redemption.

If you, Lord, keep account of sins,
Lord, who can stand?
But with you is forgiveness.
—Psalm 130:3–4

I have two younger sisters, and the three of us fought a lot while we were growing up. Sometimes it was over silly things like clothes, but other times it was about deeper issues, such as lifestyle choices or hurtful actions. Today, though, we're incredibly close. When something meaningful or difficult happens in my life, my first phone call is usually to my sisters. Our relationships wouldn't be possible if, every time I looked at them, I recalled past hurt. We've built a bond of love and trust and chosen not to keep a record of wrongs.

The psalmist reminds us today that God operates in a similar way. He knows every sin, every failure, and every missed opportunity for love in our lives. And while he could keep a perfect account, he chooses not to. Rather, in his infinite mercy, God forgives completely. He never hesitates to offer us a fresh chance to restore our relationship by beginning again.

Rest in silence with the Lord.

What would it look like to let go of the record of wrongs—either your own or someone else's—to make space for forgiveness and healing?

If you, Lord, keep account of sins,
Lord, who can stand?
But with you is forgiveness.

+ With the Lord there is mercy and fullness of redemption.

Fifth Week of Lent

+ With the Lord there is mercy and fullness of redemption.

Indeed, goodness and mercy will pursue me
all the days of my life.
—Psalm 23:6

There are two ways I tend to become too self-reliant and forget God's constant offer of grace. The first is pretty obvious: when I turn away from God through sin. I convince myself that my ways are better and fail to respond to his invitation of love. Yet even then, God's goodness and mercy remain as close as I allow them to be. God is like the father in the parable of the prodigal son, who is always ready to run toward me and welcome me home.

The second is harder to notice. Sometimes, even in my pursuit of holiness and discipleship, I start relying too much on my will and my efforts, and not enough on God's grace. I forget that I can do nothing without him and that his grace is everything. I become so focused on discipline and spiritual growth that I lose sight of the truth: It is God who pursues me first. The spiritual life isn't about earning God's love, but rather it's about perfecting our response to it. Because every act of faith, hope, or love is in response to a God who loved us first, and his goodness and mercy will pursue us all the days of our lives.

Rest in silence with the Lord.

Are you living as if you need to earn God's love, or are you allowing yourself to respond to God's constant invitation of goodness and mercy?

Indeed, goodness and mercy will pursue me
all the days of my life.

+ With the Lord there is mercy and fullness of redemption.

Fifth Week of Lent

+ With the LORD there is mercy and fullness of redemption.

> LORD, hear my prayer;
> let my cry come to you.
> —Psalm 102:2

Every Sunday at Mass during the Universal Prayer (or Prayers of the Faithful), the congregation responds to each petition with, "Lord, hear our prayer." I've often wondered—doesn't our omniscient God already hear us at all times?

The psalmist's prayer today brings clarity. First, this plea isn't questioning God's omniscience—it's affirming God's omnipotence. God can do anything, even things that seem unlikely or impossible, like responding to our needs in ways we could never expect.

Second, I've learned that when I say, "Lord, hear my prayer," it's less about whether God is listening and more about ensuring that my heart is truly calling out to him. During the Prayers of the Faithful, I challenge myself to be fully present—to pray with my whole heart, not just recite familiar words from years of habit.

Whatever you're praying for today, follow the psalmist's example. Trust that God is always listening and focus on offering him a wholehearted prayer.

Rest in silence with the Lord.

When you pray, do you trust in God's power to respond in his perfect way and timing?

> LORD, hear my prayer;
> let my cry come to you.

+ With the LORD there is mercy and fullness of redemption.

Wednesday, March 25

Fifth Week of Lent

Solemnity of the Annunciation of the Lord

+ With the Lord there is mercy and fullness of redemption.

I do not conceal your righteousness
within my heart;
I speak of your loyalty and your salvation.
—Psalm 40:11

I'll be honest—I'm not the best at keeping secrets, especially when it's good news. I remember when my sister-in-law told us she was pregnant. Even though she wanted to keep it within the family for a few more weeks, I couldn't help but share the joy with one close friend who didn't know her. My heart was overflowing with excitement! It was such a relief when we could finally announce it to the world. Maybe you're better at keeping secrets than I am, but there's something beautiful about the desire to share joy. Whether it's a new hobby, a recent accomplishment, or life-changing news, joy isn't meant to stay hidden.

While God's goodness dwells in our hearts, it should never be contained or concealed there. It's the best news we could ever carry. Let it overflow!

Rest in silence with the Lord.

How can you share the joy of God's love and faithfulness with others this week, allowing his goodness to overflow from your heart and into the lives of those around you?

I do not conceal your righteousness
within my heart;
I speak of your loyalty and your salvation.

+ With the Lord there is mercy and fullness of redemption.

Fifth Week of Lent

+ With the Lord there is mercy and fullness of redemption.

Seek out the Lord and his might;
constantly seek his face.
—Psalm 105:4

Before I was married, I spent some time on dating apps. I didn't take it too seriously, being more interested in practicing conversation and getting comfortable with dating. But of course, I was open to the possibility that I might meet my husband there!

I still remember the nerves of meeting an online match in person for the first time. I wondered if he'd look like his photos and if we'd connect in real life the way we did over messages. I especially recall one date when I arrived early at a coffee shop. Every time the door opened, I looked up, searching each face to see if it was him. Finally, he arrived, and three months later, we were engaged.

Today's psalm reminds me of that experience. God keeps his promises, but we are called to seek him out. Just as he had a plan for Abraham and his descendants, he has a plan of loving goodness for you. So never grow tired of seeking the God who loves you, because you will find him.

Rest in silence with the Lord.

Where in your life is God inviting you to seek him more intentionally, and trust in both his promises and plan for you?

Seek out the Lord and his might;
constantly seek his face.

+ With the Lord there is mercy and fullness of redemption.

Fifth Week of Lent

+ With the Lord there is mercy and fullness of redemption.

I love you, Lord, my strength,
Lord, my rock, my fortress, my deliverer.
—Psalm 18:2–3

Growing up, I was most familiar and comfortable with prayers of petition, intercession, and thanksgiving. As a young adult, as I got to know God better, I also learned praise, which glorifies God for who he is, not just for what he has done for you. But somewhat surprisingly, I'm still learning how to pray through blessing! The *Catechism* tells us in paragraph 2645, "Because God blesses the human heart, it can in return bless him who is the source of every blessing." This is exactly what today's psalm reflects.

The psalmist is essentially saying, "You saved me, God! And I love you for it!" It's about giving back to God in prayer what we owe him because of what he has done—not just saying "thank you," but proclaiming who God is to you because of his goodness in your life.

Rest in silence with the Lord.

Who is God to you today, and how can you bless him in prayer?

I love you, Lord, my strength,
Lord, my rock, my fortress, my deliverer.

+ With the Lord there is mercy and fullness of redemption.

Fifth Week of Lent

+ With the Lord there is mercy and fullness of redemption.

I will turn their mourning into joy,
I will show them compassion and have them rejoice
after their sorrows.
—Jeremiah 31:13

Recall the psalm from the first Sunday of Lent: "Give me back the joy of your salvation, and a willing spirit sustain in me" (Ps 51:14). We began this Lenten journey asking the Lord to help us rediscover the joy of life in Christ and to grant us the grace needed for the road ahead. Now, five weeks later, the Church offers us God's response through the words of Jeremiah: that he will show us the compassion we asked for, and we will rejoice again after sorrow.

God is so good! I have been praying for you to have a fruitful Lent. It's rarely an easy journey, but if you've made it this far and are reading this reflection today, give thanks to God for the willing spirit he has clearly sustained in you. Our journey isn't over yet. Tomorrow, Lent intensifies as we enter Holy Week. Personally, I almost always find Holy Week to be a struggle. Entering into Christ's Passion stirs many emotions—as it should. Whatever surfaces for you this week, hold fast to God's promise: He will turn your mourning into joy.

Rest in silence with the Lord.

How have you experienced God's compassion this Lent, and how can you let that carry you into Holy Week with trust?

I will turn their mourning into joy,
I will show them compassion and have them rejoice
after their sorrows.

+ With the Lord there is mercy and fullness of redemption.

March 29

Palm Sunday

+ LORD, in your great love, answer me.

They shake their heads at me:
"He relied on the LORD—let him deliver him;
if he loves him, let him rescue him."
—Psalm 22:8–9

The Church's tradition of a participatory reading of the Passion narrative on Palm Sunday invites us to step into the roles of various characters and reflect on how we would have acted in their place. What would I do as Peter in the courtyard? As John or Mary at the foot of the Cross? As Pilate?

Today's psalm is a profound one for these are the words Jesus quotes on the Cross when he cries out to the Father. This psalm helps us enter more deeply into his suffering, especially as we reflect on times when our own faith has been challenged. I've never heard these exact words spoken to me, and I doubt you have had them flung at you. But it's likely we all recall moments when we were mocked for believing, or when prayer seemed foolish in the eyes of others. Imagine being Jesus—mocked in the very act of rescuing the world from sin and darkness. Yet, that's the answer: God loves us so much that he sent his Son to rescue us. That's what Holy Week is all about.

Rest in silence with the Lord.

How much do you believe that God loves you? How is God inviting you to receive that love more fully this Holy Week?

They shake their heads at me:
"He relied on the LORD—let him deliver him;
if he loves him, let him rescue him."

+ LORD, in your great love, answer me.

Monday, March 30
Holy Week

+ LORD, in your great love, answer me.

I believe I shall see the LORD's goodness
in the land of the living.
—Psalm 27:13

How do you feel when a prayer doesn't get answered the way you hoped? For me, it can be challenging to maintain unwavering trust in God. Maybe something you were praying for this Lent didn't happen. Or perhaps you've been discerning a decision but still haven't found peace. Whatever you're carrying into Holy Week, *don't give up*!

God works outside the constraints of time as we perceive time. And that can be hard for us time-bound humans to grasp. But what a gift it is to lean on trust in God's timing when things don't unfold the way we wanted. If you're feeling discouraged, adopt the words of the psalmist today: "I believe I will see God's goodness in the land of the living, even if it's not right here or right now." Let this promise and hope carry you through Holy Week.

Rest in silence with the Lord.

Be honest with God about what you hoped to get out of your Lenten journey. Share your joys and your disappointments. Tell him you trust his timing and his plan.

I believe I shall see the LORD's goodness
in the land of the living.

+ LORD, in your great love, answer me.

Tuesday, March 31

Holy Week

+ Lord, in your great love, answer me.

On you I have depended since birth;
from my mother's womb you are my strength;
my hope in you never wavers.
—Psalm 71:6

I think one thing that's been lost over time in Christian culture is just how radical some of Jesus's teachings were in his time and for the early Christians. Take, for example, when Jesus taught his disciples to pray the "Our Father." Before that, it would have been unthinkable to address the God who revealed himself to Moses as "I AM" with such intimacy. Yet, for most of us today, it feels natural—even easier—to relate to God as Father rather than as the almighty Creator who spoke the heavens and the earth into existence.

No matter when your conversion or faith journey began, God has loved you from the very beginning of your existence—even before you were born. God gave you life and entrusted you to the world. As your Father, he has been with you every step of the way and has always known every choice you would make, and he has loved you through it all.

Rest in silence with the Lord.

How can remembering that God has been with you for every step of your journey help you trust more deeply in his love during Holy Week?

On you I have depended since birth;
from my mother's womb you are my strength;
my hope in you never wavers.

+ Lord, in your great love, answer me.

Holy Week

+ LORD, in your great love, answer me.

See, you lowly ones, and be glad;
you who seek God, take heart!
For the LORD hears the poor,
and does not spurn those in bondage.
—Psalm 69:33–34

Last year, during the Jubilee, Pope Francis opened a very special Holy Door at Rebibbia New Complex Prison in Rome. It was an extraordinary gesture. The Holy Father explained that he wanted to show all people that they "have the opportunity to fling open the doors to their hearts and to understand that hope never disappoints."

We are all in bondage in some way—whether bound by sin, by fear, or simply by the brokenness of our fallen world. Only God can truly set us free, and we are about to commemorate the saving mystery central to our faith as we begin the celebration of the Paschal Triduum tomorrow evening. As we prepare ourselves for these holiest of days, know that God hears you. He loves you, no matter where you find yourself, no matter what you've done. So, seek God and take heart.

Rest in silence with the Lord.

Where in your life do you feel bound by sin, fear, or struggle? Can you renew your trust that God sees you, hears you, and will rescue you?

See, you lowly ones, and be glad;
you who seek God, take heart!
For the LORD hears the poor,
and does not spurn those in bondage.

+ LORD, in your great love, answer me.

April 2
Holy Thursday

+ LORD, in your great love, answer me.

How can I repay the LORD
for all the great good done for me?
I will raise the cup of salvation
and call on the name of the LORD.
—Psalm 116:12–13

Today, we celebrate two of the greatest gifts Christ has given to his Church: the Eucharist and the priesthood. But how could we ever begin to repay such extraordinary gifts? The psalmist asks this very question and reveals a surprising answer: We don't repay God in the way we might instinctively want to. When someone gives us a gift, especially one of great value, our human tendency is to look for a way to "return the favor." But God's gifts are vast, undeserved, and freely given. All you or I can do is receive. To "raise the cup of salvation" is not an act of repayment but of humble acceptance.

Let's not burden ourselves with thoughts of how to try to repay God. Instead, lift the cup—both in the liturgy and in your heart—with full and joyful gratitude. That is the response God desires—hearts and minds open to his presence.

Rest in silence with the Lord.

Can you shift your heart from trying to repay God to opening your heart to receive his gifts, especially the Eucharist, with gratitude and humility?

How can I repay the LORD
for all the great good done for me?
I will raise the cup of salvation
and call on the name of the LORD.

+ LORD, in your great love, answer me.

April 3
Good Friday

+ LORD, in your great love, answer me.

Into your hands I commend my spirit;
you will redeem me, LORD, God of truth.
—Psalm 31:6

Have you ever felt like you hit rock bottom? I've had a few of those moments—times when all I could do was look up to heaven, through tears, and say, "I can't do this. Only you can." It's humbling and a bit heartbreaking that, sometimes, it takes reaching the very end of our strength, when the last light of hope feels like it's fading, to finally surrender everything to God.

Each year, I have a tradition of watching *The Passion of the Christ* on Good Friday. Honestly, it feels like a form of self-imposed suffering. I have to look away at times. I cry at the horror of what Jesus endured. But I choose to let myself feel the weight of it and to be overwhelmed until I reach that place of total desperation, where my heart turns back to God completely.

When we reflect on the Cross and the sins Jesus died for, it can feel heavy, even despairing. But there's only one response: surrender. Give him your whole self, just as Jesus did for love of you, and trust that the Lord will redeem you.

Rest in silence with the Lord.

What are you still holding onto at this conclusion of your Lenten journey? How is God inviting you to surrender it completely to him, trusting that he will redeem you?

Into your hands I commend my spirit;
you will redeem me, LORD, God of truth.

+ LORD, in your great love, answer me.

April 4

Holy Saturday

+ Lord, in your great love, answer me.

How varied are your works, Lord!
In wisdom you have made them all;
the earth is full of your creatures.
—Psalm 104:24

I've always found Holy Saturday to be the strangest day, and I imagine the apostles and the three Marys felt the same. As devout Jews, it was their Sabbath, a day of rest and worship. But how could the world keep turning after Jesus died? How could those who condemned him go on living while his body lay in the tomb? God truly works in mysterious ways.

Holy Saturday invites us to remember that God loved all things into existence and that nothing we do could ever diminish that love. Not even killing his Son. Not even denying him out of fear. Every person and every creature on earth is known and loved by God, and it's by that love that we endure the silence of Holy Saturday and await the light that breaks through the darkness—a light that will shine forth at the Easter Vigil tonight and spread across the world on Easter morning.

Rest in silence with the Lord.

When have you struggled to understand God's ways in your life? How can Holy Saturday remind you to trust in both God's wisdom and love, even when his plan feels hidden or mysterious?

How varied are your works, Lord!
In wisdom you have made them all;
the earth is full of your creatures.

+ Lord, in your great love, answer me.

April 5

Easter Sunday

+ Give thanks to the Lord, for he is good; his mercy endures forever.

The stone which the builders rejected
has become the cornerstone.
By the Lord has this been done;
it is wonderful in our eyes.
—Psalm 118:22–23

Easter reveals the truth we've been preparing for throughout Lent: Our prayer, sacrifices, waiting, and journey through the desert were not in vain. All throughout Lent, we've been invited to trust in God's mercy. The Cross, which seemed like defeat, becomes victory. Every moment you spent this Lent turning your heart to God, every prayer whispered in hope, every burden laid before him—*this* is the answer.

Today, we don't need to dwell on the times we've rejected Jesus from our hearts. His Resurrection proves that he can overcome anything, even our failures. Only by the power of God's love could such a miracle take place. Rejoice! The God who asked for your trust has proven faithful and that your hope was not misplaced. In the resurrected Christ, our refuge and cornerstone, God's mercy has triumphed, and he is making all things new.

Rest in silence with the Lord.

How can you live this week as a person of Easter—someone whose trust in the Lord has been answered with love?

The stone which the builders rejected
has become the cornerstone.
By the Lord has this been done;
it is wonderful in our eyes.

+ Give thanks to the Lord, for he is good; his mercy endures forever.

Emily Mae Mentock is an award-winning digital strategist, creative director, and producer passionate about evangelizing through Catholic media. As a consultant to the USCCB Committee on Evangelization and Catechesis, she leads various digital evangelization projects, including serving as creative director of Real+True and executive producer of *The Violinist: Stories of Solanus Casey*, a documentary from Formed's *Based on a True Saint* series.

Her career includes leading social media for *Verily Magazine*, launching Grotto Network at the University of Notre Dame, and overseeing strategy for the Archdiocese of Detroit. A regional Emmy winner and recipient of the Father John Catoir Social Media Evangelization Award, Mentock brings a personal, accessible approach to faith-based storytelling.

She lives in South Bend, Indiana, with her husband and serves on the Ave Maria Press Board of Directors.

Instagram: @emilymae.mentock
X: @emilymentock

Founded in 1865, Ave Maria Press,
a ministry of the Congregation of
Holy Cross, is a Catholic publishing
company that serves the spiritual and
formative needs of the Church and its
schools, institutions, and ministers;
Christian individuals and families; and
others seeking spiritual nourishment.

For a complete listing of titles from

Ave Maria Press

Sorin Books

Forest of Peace

Christian Classics

visit www.avemariapress.com